# Boot Camp for Christian Writers

I0500415

More Secrets to Getting Published— Again and Again and Again!

"Photography: Creating the Perfect Article Package"
"One Idea—Multiple Markets"
"Networking Successfully with Magazine Editors"

Carolyn Tomlin

About the Front Cover

It has been said, "A picture says a 1,000 words!" I believe they say much more! This cover photo shows my parents, Earl and Linnie McKnight Ross. It was made before their marriage in 1936 in West Kentucky on my grandmother's farm. As a writer, I know the season of the year, their happiness about being together, the country location, the license plate, the make of the car, and the time of day. But I also know...the rest of the story!

**More Secrets to Getting Published—
Again and Again and Again!
by Carolyn Tomlin**

All rights reserved.
Copyright 2012

This book or parts thereof may not be reproduced in any form, stored in a retrieval system, or transmitted in any form by any means without prior written permission of the author, except as provided by United States of America copyright law.

Author Website/blog: www.carolyntomlin.com
Book design: Ellen C. Maze, The Author's Mentor www.theauthorsmentor.com
Cover Image and Select Interior Photos Credit: Carolyn Tomlin

ISBN-13:
978-1481217842
ISBN-10:
1481217844
Also in eBook form

All scripture was utilized from the New International Version (NIV) Bible translations unless otherwise noted in the text.

PRINTED IN THE UNITED STATES OF AMERICA

Endorsement for the Boot Camp for Christian Writer

The Boot Camp for Christian Writers has helped me use my talents and skills as a writer. I'm excited about attending each workshop and look forward to learning ways to promote and market my work.

~Dr. Peggy Hamlett

The Book Camp for Christian Writers answered questions I've had for years. I can't tell you how much Carolyn and Denise mean to me and how much support you have given me in writing-to-publish. Before I started attending the workshops, I was always writing, but was growing discouraged and not going anywhere. Today, I'm a published writer.

~Adrienne Riggs

Thanks again to you and Denise for your encouragement to us as fledging writers as we attempt to capture, harness and share our hodge-podge of thoughts.

~Shirley Ferguson, *Birth Cry*

Boot Camp for Christian Writers
Carolyn Tomlin

More Secrets to Getting Published, Again and Again and Again

Section 1
"Photography: Creating the Perfect Article Package"

While writers use words to inform, entertain, educate and encourage readers, photographers depend on cameras. When these two mediums are combined, you create a winning combination most editors can't pass up! I will show you how presenting this combination to an editor can make a difference in getting an article contract—instead of a rejection letter. You'll learn how to use digital photography with an article query that will put your idea at the top of an editor's stack.

Section 2
"One Idea—Multiple Markets"

Use your research for many articles instead of just one. Research your topic once, and sell it many times! You can expand the magazine market by choosing a general topic that appeals to both Christian and secular publications. I'll help you discover how using "webbing" results in multiple sales that reach millions of people annually.

Section 3
"Networking Successfully with Magazine Editors"

Developing personal working relationships with magazine editors will increase your contacts in the publishing field and lead to more articles sold and published. I will teach you simple networking ideas that make a huge difference in your article sales. By following these techniques, you can also write for several magazines within the same company and expand your links.

Bonus!

To make writing easier, I've included some examples that will answer questions on the advantages of using digital photos when submitting a query. I'll share tips for using one basic idea and creating multiple articles from the same research and data. For me, networking tops the list as the number one approach to generating sales for the magazine market. I'll show you what works for me!

Additional pages provide space for personal thoughts as you learn from this book. The Appendix offers advice as you write-to-publish. I ask God's blessings on you as write articles that inspire, educate, inform and entertain your readers.

I believe that writing is a gift given by God. He gives us this talent and it's up to us to learn the mechanics of putting words on paper. A Bible verse that has given me hope follows:

"But those who hope in the Lord will renew their strength. They will soar on wings like eagles; they will run and not grow weary, they will walk and not be faint" (Isaiah 40:31).

"Whatever you do, work at it with all your heart, as working for the Lord, not for men… It is the Lord Christ you are serving."

~ Colossians 3:12-17 & 3:23-24

Dedication

This book is dedicated to my parents, Earl and Linnie McKnight Ross and my extended family of aunts, uncles, grandparents and other relatives. Each, in their own way, gave me encouragement and guidance that taught me lessons about living the good life.

A Personal Note to My Reader

This workbook is written especially for you—the **Boot Camp for Christian Writers®** boot campers. When you attend our all-day workshops, we are limited in time and cannot cover all the material you need. Corresponding to the workshop title, these books provide a deeper and more advanced study of the chosen topics. Designed to be used at home and when you have time to reflect, these books are a follow up to this seminar. After each section, space is provided for you to interact with the information. Use the additional pages to develop your own ideas by following the examples and format.

Writers can reach millions of readers annually through magazines. Writing can not only change the life of others—it changes your life, also! Our Boot Campers are people just like you. Perhaps you've thought of writing for years—but haven't started. Or, if you're like me, I thought no one would want to publish my work. Young people discover that writing can lead to interesting careers. Single parents earn extra money in this stay-at-home job. Seniors write their memoirs. And others turn an avocation into a vocation. You see, writing has no age limit. There's no retirement until "you" decide it's time to quit. An editor really doesn't care what you look like—or if you stay home and work in your PJs all day, or even if you comb your hair!

I've often said, "When the Lord knows it's best for me over there, in heaven instead of this earth, I hope someone finds me at my computer with my index finger on the "Send" key of my computer. And that my last manuscript "did" go through!

It is my prayer that writing will do for you—what it has done for me. And that you will develop a passion for writing and write articles and books that make a difference in the lives of others. May God bless you as you write for Him.

~With all my best wishes, Carolyn Tomlin

Table of Contents

Introduction

When Denise George and I first thought of planning a writing workshop in 2009, we were both established writers. I had over 3,000 published articles and 6 books, and Denise had published about 1,200 magazine articles and over 2 dozen books. This being said, we knew what worked for us. But as we scheduled our Boot Camp for Christian Writers, we learned so much from those who attended.

We wondered what would happen if we took what we knew and learned from others who shared their knowledge, and combined this information in a seminar? Would people want to learn more about the mechanics of writing-to-publish? And would they share their skills and talents with others?

Today, over 1,500 people have either attended our workshops or had contact with us. We are family! Because we can not present writing-to-publish workshops all over the United States and foreign countries, we have published a series of workbooks on writing. The workbooks are translated into all major languages and are available as paperback books and are also on Kindle e-books.

Prison Fellowship Ministries, started by Chuck Colson, is part of our Boot Camp for Christian Writers® ministry. They are our newest family members. The following quotation helps me focus on this unique ministry:

"People want to be appreciated, not impressed.

They want to be regarded

as human beings,

not mere

sounding boards

for other people's egos.

They want to be treated

as an end in themselves,

not as a means

toward the gratification

of another's vanity."

~Sydney J. Harris

Shared knowledge is like throwing a pebble into still water. As the pebble is thrown in, ripples form, and in a matter of seconds, more and more ripples continue until they reach the bank. It's true of teaching. Sharing information with others and participating in the lives of those we meet makes life worth living.

Section 1: Photography: Creating the Perfect Article Package

While writers use words to inform, entertain, educate and encourage readers, photographers depend on cameras. When these two mediums are combined, you create a winning combination most editors can't pass up! I will show you how presenting this combination to an editor can make a difference in getting an article contract—instead of a rejection letter. You'll learn how to use digital photography with an article query that will put your idea at the top of an editor's stack.

Which comes first, the article idea or the photo? Or going back to the age-old question: Which came first—the chicken or the egg? There is no one correct answer. For me, sometimes I have the idea, write the article, then either make the photo or use one from my files. On another occasion, I'll snap a digital photo and this image will turn my creative juices on. And immediately, it's that moment when I see the article outline develop in my mind. Words become sentences. Sentences become paragraphs. Paragraphs become an article. All because of a photo that inspired me to write! It's times like this when I say: *I can't not write.*

A following quote applies to photos—just as it applies to these thoughts.
"Any time a thought, sentence, or paragraph inspires you or opens up your thinking, you need to capture it, like a butterfly in a net, and later release it into your own field of consciousness." ~Steve Chandler

Difference between Writers and Photographers

I believe creativity is necessary for both a writer and a photographer. A writer uses letters of the alphabet to draw word pictures. A photographer uses a camera to create visual images for the mind. When combined, you have a package that most editors can't turn down.

Writers…

- Rely on words to tell a story.
- Deliver a message.
- Explain a situation.
- Educate.
- Inform.
- Encourage.
- Inspire.

Photographers…

- Use a camera as a means of communication with the audience.
- Allow the viewer to "see" through your eyes.
- Introduce the non-reader to the world.
- Eliminate the language barrier.

Memoir about a Photograph: Mother, Daddy and the Old Car

What do you see when you look at an old family photo? Do you notice joy or sadness in their expressions? What are the details, other than the people in the photo? How are they dressed? Old family pictures give us a glimpse into the life and personality of people. Use those in your family to write your own story. This is mine.

One of my favorite family pictures shows my parents, Earl and Linnie McKnight Ross, sitting on the fender of a 1930 or 1931 Chevrolet Coupe. Made before they married in 1936, my father drove his bride-to-be, to West Kentucky to meet his family before they married in May of that year. Linnie lived in Malesus, Tennessee—a small rural community about five-miles south of Jackson. Marrying at age 26, they were a little older than many of their friends when they tied-the-knot.

Mother's hair was dark brown with a small amount of curl. From her Scot-Irish ancestors, she inherited her fair complexion. Dad, quite the opposite. He inherited dark skin and very fine, straight- black hair from his Indian blood-line.

Obviously, the photo was made in warm weather— either late spring, summer or early fall. With their wedding date of May 14, 1936, I assume it was the spring of that year. Their choice of clothing also indicated the season. Dad was wearing white clothing with his sleeves rolled up. In the 1930s, men didn't usually wear short-sleeve shirts. Mother is wearing a summer dress, with plaid fabric cut on the bias. As all clothing was homemade, she certainly made this dress as part of her trousseau. Matching plaids on the bias required a talented seamstress! Years later, I recall seeing this garment tucked away in a trunk—one where she kept important mementos of her life.

Owning a car was unusual. Dad had just returned home from the Army after completing two years in Panama. Did he save his soldier pay to buy the Chevy Coupe? One thing's for sure, he didn't buy a car or any large purchase until he had cash to pay in full. He continued this character trait all his life. I recall Mother saying they only had one spare tire for the car. Returning to her home in Malesus,

Tennessee, south of Jackson, one tire had a blowout and Dad put on the spare. A few miles down the road, another tire blew. They drove the last twenty miles on a rim, making a lot of noise and frightening chickens along the route. Drawing this attention was embarrassing to Mother. It never seemed to bother Dad.

The picture also indicated a county setting. A tobacco barn, with its high roof for smoking the harvested plant, is in the background. The weathered building was still standing when I as a child. It's the place my dad's mother, who I called "Grandmother" allowed me to milk my first cow. Old Bessie didn't like just anybody milking her. She took one look at who was trying to tease the milk from her teats, gave a loud Mooo...flipped my face with her long tail and kicked over the bucket. Needless to say, Grandmother wasn't very happy!

The shadow of the person taking the picture was my father's younger 6-year-old sister, Mary Frances. Using an old Brownie Box camera she "pointed" and "clicked." By the size of her shadow, it is late afternoon and the sun is setting in the West. My parents are squinting and looking into the bright sun that meets their eyes. The pose is perfect; both with their right legs crossed over the left. Unplanned, I'm sure.

And about that car... My parents continued to drive the automobile for several years. Because of the Great Depression and the economic condition, jobs were hard to find. Therefore, my family lived with her mother and sister in the house we called "The Home Place." After saving as much money as possible and tearing down a couple of old houses for the lumber, my father had "almost" enough to build a small home. But not quite! That's where the car comes in. He found a man who would pay him $300 for the car. With this additional cash, my father could complete the dwelling. And with this amount, they could be out on their own.

But for me, I loved that old car. One of my first memories is of my father accepting an envelope with cash, shaking hands with the buyer and him driving away—as I ran after the car begging my father to get it back.

I often wonder if the new owners took care of the car and kept it polished. Perhaps, today, it's in an antique car museum, where people come and see the automobiles of yesterday. And if cars could talk, this car would tell of the time it helped… a young family… build a home.

Why Add Photos?

Do photos really make a difference in publishing for the magazine market? Yes! Ask a writer who has a stack of rejections compared to one who has been successful in publishing. If the writer who has published submitted quality photos and the rejected writer did not include these—you have your answer. Offering a package (the article and supporting photos) gives you an edge over others. In a competitive market, writers need to focus on what works for others and apply these ideas to their own style.

Use these suggestions to build your "acceptance pile" as compared to your "rejections pile." Keep these suggestions in mind as you seek photography assignments.

- A photo package shows you are serious about your work. It demonstrates you know the magazine and are familiar with the type photos used in previous editions.

- A photo package is more economical for the magazine. If a writer makes their own photos, the editor doesn't have to waste time or money sending someone on staff. Unless you are well-known, it's unlikely the magazine will pay a professional photographer to fly to Moscow, Russia, to photograph St. Basil's Cathedral.

- A photo package adds authenticity to your work. It shows the editor you were there—climbing the Great Wall of China. Personally, I take photos of people, places and things. Focusing on faces that show character. Facial lines and wrinkles tell their own story. If you're in one of the photos, make it an action shot. Ask a friend or colleague to snap your photo—and return the favor.

- Use photos to reveal the five senses—seeing, hearing, tasting, smelling, and touching. You'll weave these senses into your article to make it come alive.

- Photos help you organize material. They recall the people you met, the places you visited, and the activities you participated in. When you return home, organize your photos in a web folder. Do this immediately after a trip while the information is fresh on your mind.

- Use photos to make a chronological outline of your trip. Notes in a journal and photos bring back ideas you might forget when you begin writing.

- Photos show the "before" and "after" of a how-to article. For example, for a garland of natural materials, make a photo of the assembled material with the tools needed for the project. Showing the process of making the craft would be helpful to the reader. Include the finished product. An example of a "then" and "now" article could show a person as a baby or young child and as they look today.

Combining Words and Pictures

We learn in different ways. When you provide a photo with the written text, the reader retains the information. Look at these four combinations of both words and pictures.

Writers Use Words to Educate

Located in Pushkin, near St. Petersburg, Russia, the Hermitage is part of Catherine's Palace. Built in the early 1700s, this ornate blue stucco building is used as an art gallery for thousands of pieces of Russian art.

Photographers Use Pictures to Educate

Writers Use Words to Inform

The gray squirrel is common to all parts of the United States. Considered a wild animal of the woods, this hard-working animal, a relative of the rodent family, spends much of its time searching for food and preparing a habitat.

Photographers Use Pictures to Inform

Writers Use Words to Entertain

What makes this photo funny? We don't expect a dog to be at the table with a napkin around his neck. Neither do we expect the dog to eat from china plates or drink from a crystal goblet. However, Rocky is anxious to enjoy this milk bone in return for sitting still for a moment.

Photographers Use Pictures to Entertain

Writers Use Words to Encourage

During the late 1930s, Stalin ordered that all the bells be removed from the Russian Orthodox churches. Bells encourage people to serve God and to attend church services. The churches were usually left standing, but the doors were bricked up and the bells removed.

Photographers Use Pictures to Encourage

Articles + Photo(s) = CONTRACTS

Submit Digitals with a Query

When I email a query letter, I always send three to four digitals that support the article. This gives the editor a visual image of how the article will be formatted and what photos the graphic designer can use. By sending digitals, this creates a professional opinion of your work.

Correspondence from an Editor

What happens after you correspond with an editor? Perhaps you've emailed your query and digital photos, but you haven't received a response. Check the *Writer's Market* or online guidelines for the length of time until you will be notified. If the time frame is 6 weeks, and you haven't heard, email a brief note inquiring about the status of your query. Always speak in a courteous tone and voice. You may receive one of the following:

1. Please submit your article and photo package... (YES)

2. Our editorial panel would like to see more photos describing places for families to visit while in... (MAYBE)

3. After careful review, our editorial board does not believe we are the best magazine for your article idea and photo package. However, we appreciate your thinking of us. Please feel free to submit other article ideas and photo packages in the future. (NO, BUT TRY AGAIN.)

I have a practice of writing a brief thank-you note or email for each rejection. In this note I express my appreciation for the editor reviewing my article/photos. After I've reviewed additional back copies and studied the magazine, I will submit another idea soon. In a week or two, I send another submission. Breaking into a new market for articles and photos may require several tries---but it's worth the effort.

Dealing With Acceptance or Rejection

1. Don't take it personally.

2. Learn from rejection.

3. Research more back copies of the magazine and photos used in the issue.

4. Never argue with an editor or try to convince him/her that your article/photos should be published. One editor actually had a writer say, "Jesus told me to send these photos. Don't change a thing."

Why Photos are Rejected

- Unclear images. Movement, blurred, and unclear.

- Wrong dot-per-inch (DPI). Editors prefer 300 dpi as they are suitable for cover photos.

- Off center (apply to rules of thirds). Think of a dog running off the photo, or a ship sailing off the side of the picture.

- Shadows from the photographer seen in the photo.

- Photo credit was not provided. Learn to supply your own. List yourself: such as: Photo credit: Carolyn Tomlin

- Photo image not mention in the article. Photos support the text.

- Noon sun does not produce quality images. Use early morning or late afternoon. A cloudy day provides more hours to shoot.

Examples of Rejected Photos

1. Unclear image

2. Out of focus

3. Proportion wrong

4. Off center

Digital photography has changed the way I once filed photographs. A few years ago, I purchased rolls of 35 mm. film, shot images, and hopefully, had a few quality prints. For those considered saleable, I kept in loose-leaf binders or plastic slide holders. Today, I return from a photo shoot, download the images to my computer, and make necessary changes. When I need a digital photo to support an article, or to catch an editor's attention when submitting a query letter, I bring up the photo, attach it to the email, and press "send." Times have changed!

Another suggestion that works for me: Each time you're out shooting a particular topic, download to your computer that day. Make a folder and a sub-folder

Because I take many photos, I need a filing system so I can locate digitals quickly. For example, take the topic of "Animals." These could be divided into:

Animals

People

The Five Senses

Animals

Pets	Farm	Zoo	Wild
Dogs	Cows	Bears	Squirrels
Cats	Horses	Zebra	Rabbit

Family	International People
Parents	Russian
Children	Chinese
Grandparents	Cuban

The Five Senses

Hearing	Smelling	Tasting	Touching	Seeing
Thunder	Roses	Coffee	Cat's fur	Sunset
Parade	Perfume	Lemons	Hair	Traffic

Finding the Best Photo

Photography is a skill —and a skill can be learned. Use these tips for shooting quality photos.

- Create your own—but use ideas from others.

- Look at photos from other photographers. For example, you plan to take a trip to China. You want a photo of the Great Wall. Find another one that meets your requirements, and stand in the same location and capture the image.

- Study postcards before your trip. Do you see images you will need for your article? Your photo will be similar—but different in some aspects.

- Study the magazine where you plan to submit an article/photo package. How are photos used in the publication?

An idea just came to you. Jot it down here:

_____

_____

_____

_____

_____

_____

_____

_____

Titles sell articles. I often use a photo to create a catchy article title. Look at the following photos. Which of the titles would interest an editor?

1. Shoe trees: A Southern Folk Art

2. American's Strange Trees

3. Shoe Trees: A Trend on America's Highways

Why did you choose this title?_____

_____

1. Pets Like to Travel

2. Pet Carriers for Comfort and Safety

3. 10 Tips for Traveling With Pets

Why did you choose this title?_____

_____

Look at the following photos. Write three article titles that would support the photo.

1. _____

2. _____

3. _____

1. _____

2. _____

3. _____

1. _____

2. _____

3. _____

Reverse the Process: Article Title—Photo

Now use the reverse process. Pretend an editor has assigned you an article title. It's up to you to develop the perfect photo-package that will give you a contract with this magazine. Think outside the box. Be creative in using your talents to provide photos that support the article. List four photos that catch an editor's eye.

1. Article Title: Childhood Obesity: How can Ministers to Children Make a Difference? (Example: Consider photos of healthy food, children involved in physical activity, hiking as a family as photo ideas.)

a. _____   b._____

c. _____   c._____

2. Visit *Monticello*: Home of Thomas Jefferson

a. _____   b._____

c._____   d._____

Living the Good Life

a. _____   b._____

c._____   d._____

Camping: A Growing Trend Among Today's Families

a._____   b._____

c._____   d._____

The Secret Holocaust Diaries: The Untold Story of Nonna Bannister is a true Holocaust story of the diaries kept by a young Russian girl. Denise George and I served as contributors and co-authored the diary. One reason for the success of this book is the photographs Nonna saved in a little ticking pillow tied around her waist and under her dress while in the prison camps of Germany. Her father, Yevgeny, an amateur photographer, enjoyed making pictures of his family and friends. Made with an old German camera, these 1 X 1-inch negatives survived the war. This was unusual as most families lost all possessions. Feodosija, Nonna's maternal grandmother, believed that if anyone could survive this horrible war, her granddaughter, Nonna could. Therefore, she entrusted the young girl with the family documents and negatives before she boarded the train to travel to a German prison camp.

These photographs are part of what makes the book a success. Readers relate to photos. As they read the text, they picture in their mind the different individuals included in the story. The images represent the thousands of people throughout the world whose Holocaust story was never told. And the pictures add authenticity to the book.

This is the last known photo of Nonna's family. Made about 1935, the photo shows her brother, Anatoly; Nonna; her mother, Anna; and her father, Yevgeny. This photo was made before Anatoly left for school in St. Petersburg (in order to keep him safe from Stalin's youth group). Nonna never saw him again.

Notes from Section I:

Section 2: One Idea—Multiple Markets

Use your research for many articles instead of just one article. Research your topic once, and sell it many times! You can expand the magazine market by choosing a general topic that appeals to both Christian and secular publications. I'll help you discover how using "webbing" results in multiple sales that reach millions of people annually. Remember that each magazine goes to a different audience. As you research the market, create the perfect title for your magazine article. Don't re-invent the wheel. Choose a title and article that match the tone of the publication in which you want to write.

Before words appear on your computer or from a handwritten pad, research takes place. After a writer has spent hours researching a topic, collecting data, interviewing contacts—well, you want as many articles as possible from the same basic material. You can not sell the same article to multiple markets. But you can do this: use some of the same research, data, and contact information to write numerous articles with a different slant. How? By knowing the magazine and knowing the audience (as described in *Book Camp for Christian Writers,* Book 4, Section III and Section IV). You'll increase your sales as you submit to a variety of magazine markets.

Use these different approaches for finding multiple ideas from the same research. These ideas will increase your writing credits in a variety of publications.

1. Webbing: Brainstorming Multiple Ideas

Webbing works best for me. When I decide on a central topic, I write this word in the center of a page. This becomes the spokes of a wheel, and the spokes become subtopics generating from the main topic (the word you wrote in the center of the page). Off the subtopics, I write more sub-subtopics. Each of these could become an article. If you ever find yourself without writing ideas, use this approach:

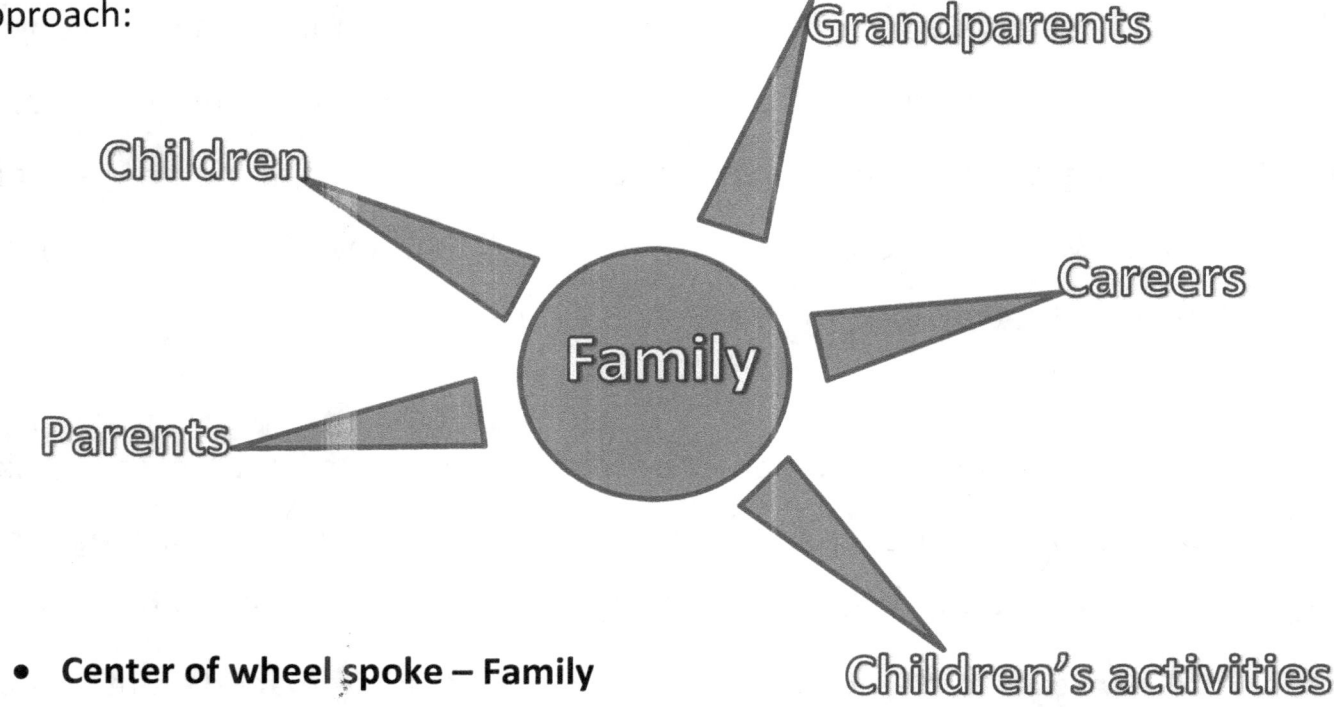

- **Center of wheel spoke – Family**

   Subtopics: Parents—Children—Grandparents—Careers—Children's

   Activities: Take the subtopic *Children*, and use school activities, friends, homework, and church involvement. Under the topic of *Friends*, use boy/girl relationships, ways to teach appreciation for another culture, and peer pressure.

   Any of the above topics can be used for a separate article. You may find research, data, or interviews that support more than one topic or sub-topic--all under the topic of "Family."

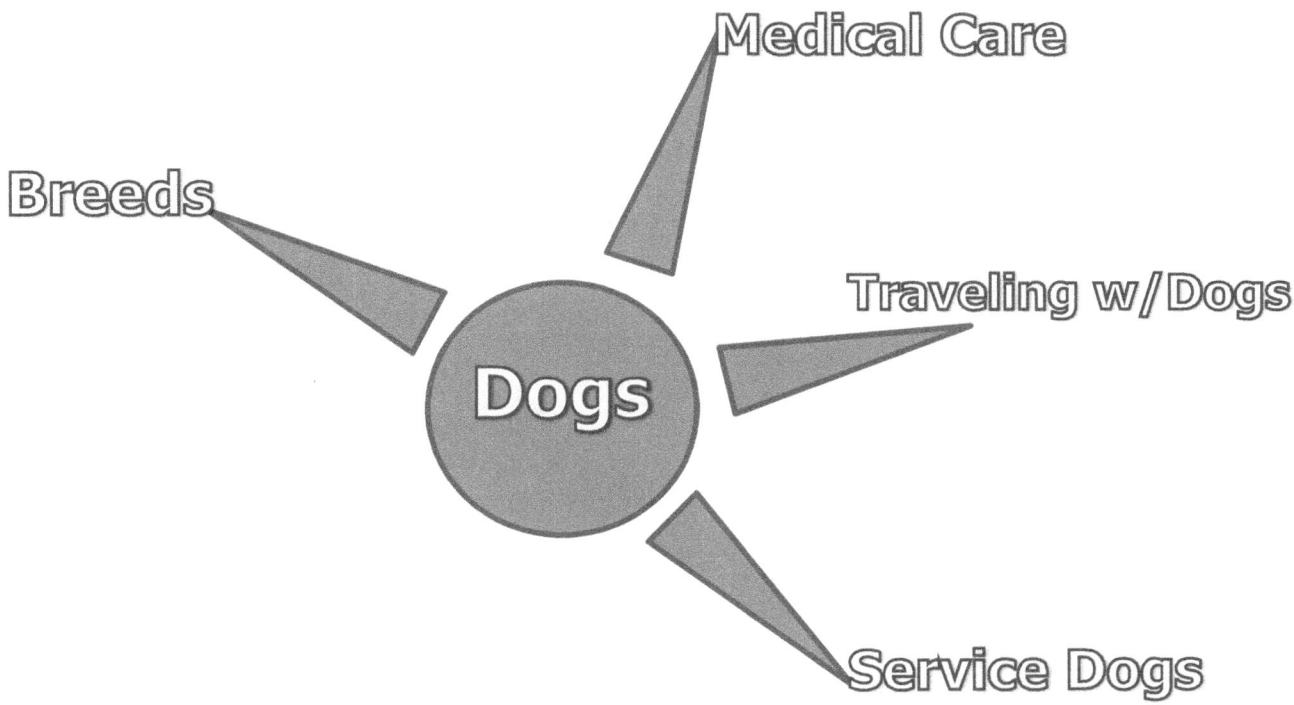

- **Center of Wheel Spoke—*Dogs***

   Subtopics—Breeds of dogs, medical care, traveling with dogs, service dogs

   Sub-Subtopics –traveling with dogs—private automobile, plane, medical records, basic needs (food and water), and safety from extreme heat or cold.

Choose a topic of interest. Make your own web design by the space below:

2. A Tree: Another Idea for Generating Ideas

Another approach is to think of the structure of a tree. The roots are the topic, the trunk is the subtopic, and the branches are the sub-subtopics.

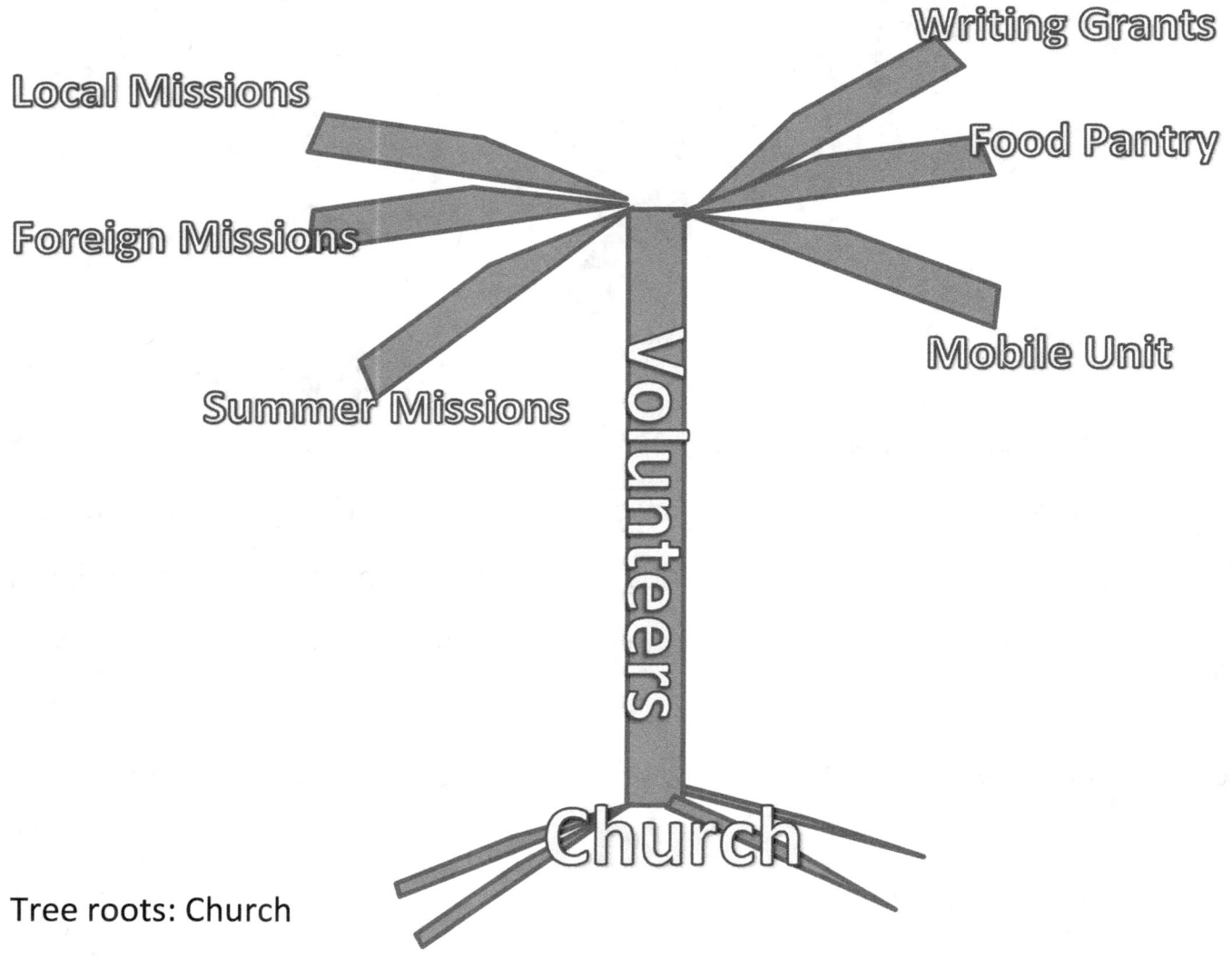

Tree roots: Church

Trunk: Volunteers

Branches: Summer missions, foreign missions, local/community missions, writing grants for faith-based projects, food pantry, mobile unit to serve meals in disaster areas, medical personnel needed in disaster areas.

You can write articles on any of the above by using some of the basic information for the topic, "Church."

Choose a topic of interest.

Write your ideas on a tree form, using the roots, trunk, and branches:

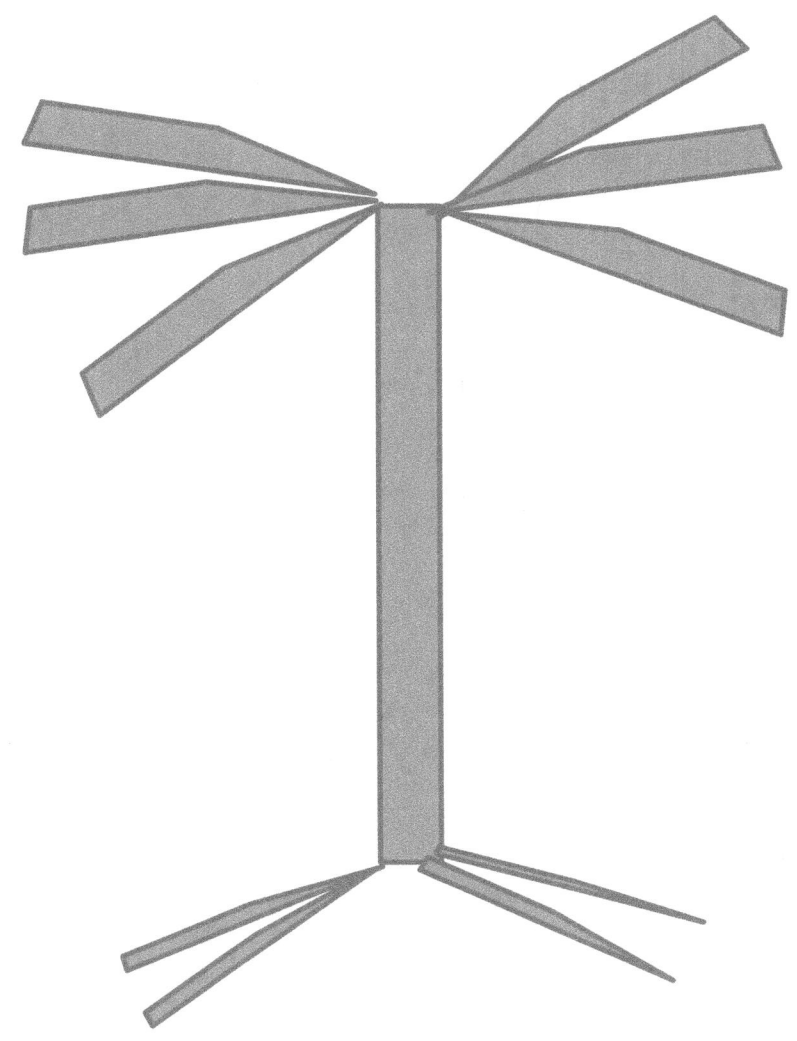

When you use webbing or a tree structure, practice the following:

- Choose a broad topic —Select a topic that you would like to know more about. If you plan to stay with this subject for several articles, it should be one of interest.

- Narrow the topic—Again, use the "keyhole" effect. Don't try to cover too many ideas within the same article. It's best to divide the material into two articles instead of packing too much into one article. When I query an editor I often suggest Part I and Part II instead of one long article.

- Expand ideas—If you can't come up with your own ideas, invite a writer friend to brainstorm thoughts with you. Soon, your mind will be overflowing with original ideas.

- Keep a list of ideas for future articles—If you're like me, there is no way you can write or market ideas for all your sub-topics. Write these ideas and keep them in a folder on your computer for future reference. But what if you want to use these ideas soon? Depending on how much time you devote to writing, fill out a monthly calendar with daily or weekly articles. For many years I set a goal or writing 300 articles annually. Today, with speaking and writing books, I publish an average of about 150 magazine articles each year. If you write daily, you can take one topic and write many articles from the same research.

- When I can't come up with ideas, I go walking. By myself, I'm inspired by the natural world God created. Are there clouds in the sky? What words describe the glorious sunset? Did I hear a bird calling from a nearby tree? What smells are present as I walk? Does my clothing make me aware of textures that touch my skin? All my senses are at work as I walk and listen as God speaks to me. And I return home with several fresh ideas for turning into articles.

3. Photos: Let Pictures Tell Their Own Story

Photos are a different way to generate ideas with multiple markets. With this form for finding ideas, you already have a starting place. For example, look at the following photo. Using the cover photo, articles could come from studying the picture and researching the various elements. Look at the following suggestions for possible articles.

3-a. Article Ideas from Photos of People

On a personal note, this photo used on the front cover is a favorite one I have of my parents. Made before they married in 1936, I see the love that lasted 48 years until my father's death. They survived the Great Depression, World War II, the death of their first-born child, raising two girls, and were able to enjoy their grandchildren. Their life was not easy—by any means. From my parents and grandparents, I learned how to live the "Good Life" by loving God, loving people, working hard, and staying happy. It works! I know!

Article Ideas:

- Eight Ideas for a Happy Marriage
- 10 Ideas for Living the Good Life
- Antique Cars: The Stories They Could Tell
- Clothing Styles of the Early 1900s.

By looking at this photo, write three additional article titles that might come from this picture.

1._____

2._____

3._____

An idea just came to you. Jot it down here:

_____

_____

_____

_____

_____

_____

_____

_____

_____

3-b. Article Ideas from Sunsets

Two of my favorite natural wonders are sunrises and sunsets. All are different. On a late afternoon, after the sun has shone brightly most of the time, ribbons of clouds appear, and the sunset is awesome! Looking at the western sky, I see colors of red, orange, yellow, mauve, purple, gold, and almost all shades of the rainbow. I'm also reminded of the old saying, "Red sky at night—sailors' delight. Red sky in the morning, sailors take warning!" Since the beginning of time, writers have used the sun to put thoughts into words. I encourage you to read Emily Dickenson's poem: "I'll Tell You How the Sun Rose—A Ribbon at a Time!"

Article Ideas:

- Sunsets Are All Different—Just Like People

- Sunsets Predict Changing Weather

- 5 Ways Sunsets Ease Stressful Living

- Reflecting on Sunsets Through Poetry

By looking at this photo, write three additional article titles that might come from this picture of a sunset.

1._____

2._____

3._____

3-c. Article Ideas from Travel Locations

Traveling allows a writer to expand his or her knowledge of the world—the people, places and things. While on a recent trip to China, I climbed the Great Wall near Beijing. While looking out at one of the stone openings, I reflected on the warriors who stood in this same location over 2,000 years ago. What were they thinking? How did this structure affect me as I stood in the exact same place?

Article Ideas:

- The Great Wall: One of the Wonders of the World

- Walls Keep People In—And Keep People Out

- What Type "Wall" Guards Your Life?

- Sacrifices That Builders of Walls Made

By looking at this photo of the Great Wall, create your own article titles:

1._____

2._____

3._____

3-d. Article Ideas from "Then" and "Now" Photos

Life along the Yangtze River in China is very different from that of a modern city in China. Farmers who live along the Yangtze have a simple, uncomplicated life. Houses consist of simple structures. A single horse helps plow the hillside vegetable garden that rises up from the muddy Yangtze. A few chickens and a cow provide for the family. Life is simple and unhurried.

In modern Shanghai, life is very different. Noise from traffic fills the air. Shoppers walk on crowded streets. Bright neon lights flash after dark. People hurry back and forth from crowded apartments as they go to work.

Article ideas that reach multiple markets may include:

1. China: "Then" and "Now"

2. Lifestyles of Country Living as Compared to City Dwellers

3. Why I Chose a Simple Country Lifestyle in China? Or, Why I Chose a Busy City Lifestyle in China.

After comparing the two photos, write 3 article titles that could go to multiple markets.

1._____

2._____

3._____

Suggestions That Work for Me!

Titles often make a difference in landing a magazine article contract for multiple markets. And yes, you can publish for many different markets in a variety of fields. These ideas have made a difference in my number of article sales:

- Sleep on an idea. Allow your dreams to turn an idea into several articles. Think about the article before bedtime. Keep a pad and pen near you on a bedside table. If you wake up with a great idea, writing one or two words can help you remember it until morning.

- Be professional and always courteous. However, this is no place to be submissive. Believe in yourself and so will others.

- Never give up! If you don't succeed, try again. If you receive a rejection on an article idea, write a letter or email to the editor thanking him or her for reviewing your query or manuscript. State that you will review back issues and study the magazine again, and that you will submit another idea in the near future. It may take several tries, but if you know the magazine and know the reader, you will be successful. Of course, you must write a query that explains (1) what the article is about (2) how you will cover the material (3) why it's an article that fits the magazine and reader, and (4) why you are the person to write the article. (See *Boot Camp for Christian Writers*, Book 4, Section 3 on writing query letters.)

- Know current trends on the topic you choose. READ, READ, READ. Writers should keep updated on trends that relate to the topic they plan to write.

- Report the latest data and research information available. With the Internet available for research, writing from home has never been easier.

- Trust God to help you. Have faith you will be successful. Matthew 21:22 reads, "If you believe, you will receive whatever you ask for in prayer."

Crossover Articles for the Christian and Secular Market

Writers who know the magazine and know the audience (the readers of the magazine) have an advantage of writing for both the Christian and secular market. Many secular magazines allow writers to add inspirational articles, and some even allow a Scripture verse included. When you search a new magazine, look for those that include articles on faith. Make a list of these publications. Then, as you brainstorm article ideas, create some for the secular and some for the Christian market. Change the focus, but use the same research for both. Multiple markets lend themselves to inspirational, how-to-do, travel, interview, personal experience, and other types of articles. Often the change is very small. Perhaps a Scripture verse, a new title, and a few words changed will make the difference in the magazine to which you submit.

Promote Your Published Book through Multiple Magazine Articles

One of the easiest ways to market your book is through the magazine market. One magazine article can reach thousands of readers. Think of the subject of the book as an umbrella. Each article falls under the umbrella and is part of the subject, yet is distinct in some way.

Dozens of magazine articles came from *The Secret Holocaust Diaries: The Untold Story of Nonna Bannister* (co-authored by Carolyn Tomlin and Denise George). By knowing the magazine and the audience, we have published numerous articles, and given presentations that reach schools, universities, libraries, churches, and civil clubs. You can promote your book in the same way.

These articles are only a few that support *The Secret Holocaust Diaries: The Untold Story of Nonna Bannister.*

- The Role of Women in the Prison Camps

- Forming Friendships: Survival Techniques Used During the Holocaust

- The Unspoken Secret: Life in the Prison Camps

- Strong Family Bonds Build Character

- Language Skills: How One Girl Survived the Holocaust

- The Role of Missionaries After the War

- A Story That Reflects the Life of Thousands

With all the work that goes into article writing, think of ways you can use the same data, research, and basic information to turn one topic or subject into multiple articles. You'll reach more readers, and your message will go to the world.

Notes from Section II:

Section 3: Networking Successfully with Magazine Editors

Developing personal working relationships with magazine editors will increase your contacts in the publishing field, and lead to more articles sold and published. I will teach you simple networking ideas that make a huge difference in your article sales. By following these techniques, you can also write for several magazines within the same company and expand your links.

In addition, Section 3 includes the following:

- How to develop personal working relationships with magazine editors.
- How to increase your contacts.
- How to publish and sell more articles.
- Learn simple networking ideas.
- How to sell to several magazines published by the same company.

Does Networking Make a Difference?

Webster's Dictionary defines "networking" as using a set of connections, arrangements, associations, a group, or a set of contacts. Synonyms include meeting people, making contacts, exchanging ideas, and interacting with others. Writers would do well to remember this definition! In my opinion, networking is one of the most important factors in reaching multiple markets. One satisfied editor tells another publication about your professional work. Or, if several magazines are published by the same company, editors talk about their writers around the water cooler. What will they say about "you" as a writer? Hopefully, they'll share words like the following:

- This is one writer who always meets our deadline.
- If a change is needed, I know he will respond within 24 hours.
- If I have to reject an article—it's no big deal!
- When I need a new idea on an old topic, I can depend on this writer for a fresh slant.

Or, does the editor share these statements about your work?

- We covered this topic two years ago. Didn't the writer check back issues?
- I've saved space for this contracted article. The deadline passed two weeks ago. I wonder if the writer plans to send it in?
- I hate to reject this writer's article again. But it doesn't meet the needs of our magazine or our readers.
- This manuscript was addressed to an editor that left our company a year ago.

Quotes on the Value of Networking

"The key to success in life is using the good thoughts of wise people."

~Leo Tolstoy

"We make a living by what we get. We make a life by what we give."

~Winston Churchill

We learn from others. Writers who develop a strong working relationship with several editors can sharpen their skills and become a person that an editor calls on often. When an editor continues to offer you contracts, you are considered part of their "stable of writers."

When I first started writing, Charlie Warren, then the editor of *HomeLife* Magazine, offered to show me how to write an article. The first draft needed some changes—a lot of changes. Charlie said, "If you'll allow me to help you, I think you will turn into one of the writers we call on regularly." So, within a few days I received my manuscript in the SASE (self-addressed stamped envelope) I had included. I felt I was in grade school again when I saw the article! He had taken a red pen and make changes and notations all over the paper. In fact, it dripped blood!

I'll never forget this act of generosity he gave to a novice writer. Instead of a stamp of rejection, this kind editor showed me "what- to-do" and "how" the article should be written. I took his advice and re-submitted the story, and it was published.

Another editor gave me words a writer loves to hear. One of my goals was to write for Moose River Publishing Company—a publisher that produced eight magazines each month, with several of them having regional publications. When I first started writing for Moose River Publishing Company, editor Bob Montgomery said, "We will keep you as busy as you want to be!" That's music to a writer's ears! If you really are serious about writing to publish, you'll understand this statement.

Getting Started: Networking with Editors

During the last 24 years, I have worked with dozens of editors. I can honesty say, we've had a positive working relationship—that is, except with one. This woman was very critical of my article, and jumped on her soapbox to defend her actions. Instead of evaluating my work, she moved on to what was wrong with the world, people in general, and the government. I decided I didn't need this, so instead of adding fuel to the fire, I marked her off as a person I didn't want to work with. This is one of the great things about free-lance work. You work with people "you" choose to work with. Oh yes, I also cut rejection letters into a 4-piece note pad!

Writers need editors; editors need writers. These suggestions make for a positive writer-editor relationship.

- Read the editor's column in each issue. You'll discover the editor's "likes" or "dislikes," and write accordingly. Consider the editor's age as to topics of interest. Are they young parents? Or grandparents?

- Check the archives or back copies as to their area of interest. I know of one editor who loves stories about horses and dogs. However, an article about a bird would never make the cut. How does a writer know these things? Again, read back copies. If you want to write an article on birds, check to see how many articles focus on winged creatures. If you find none, you have your answer.

- Timing is everything—well, almost. What if the editor hasn't had her morning coffee? Or, what if your manuscript is the last one in the stack to be read that day? Picture this: She is tired. Her eyes feel weak from too much reading. She's watching the clock—ready to go home. Guess what? The manuscript that you think is one of your best—goes in the rejection pile. These are factors a writer has no control over. My advice: Try again. And again, and again—until you receive a letter of acceptance!

- Learn simple networking ideas. Talk to other writers. What works for them? What doesn't?

- Be courteous, but assertive. If a rejection letter arrives, don't take it personally. If the editor took time to pen in some reasons, take this as a "positive" no. Or, if the editor says, "Try another slant," or "Keep trying," follow through with another idea, soon!

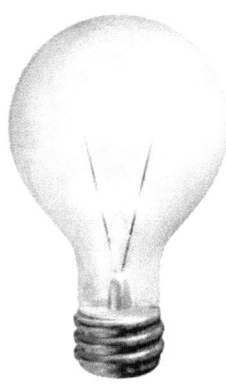

Tip # 1. Send Your Best

- Make every type of communication an example of your best work.

- Proof-read.

- Use spell-check, but don't depend on this feature to catch all mistakes. Did you really intend to type "know" or "no?"

- What if you made a mistake on the first draft and you've hit "send?" Follow up with a second edition, explaining an error you discovered. Don't over apologize.

Tip # 2. Do Your Research

- Write a complete query when working with a new publication.

- Conduct current research and data.

- Show the editor that you know the magazine. An editor will know if you're unfamiliar with the type of article you query.

- Understand the reader or audience.

Tip # 3. Keep Communications Professional

- Check on the query or manuscript status if necessary. Email and say, "I'm checking on the status of (give title of article) that was submitted on (give date). Thank the editor for reviewing your work. Know the time-frame of when you can expect an answer. If you haven't heard by this time, wait another week, and write a courteous email.

- If you do not receive a response to your email, consider this a "No" or a rejection. Let it drop and move on to another article idea.

- If an editor calls you on your home phone, act in a professional manner. Try to find a quiet room that is free from a barking dog, children crying, or the doorbell ringing.

Tip # 4. Avoid Deadline Drama

- Don't overload yourself.
- Keep a calendar of due dates. I note the deadline on my calendar about 2 weeks prior to when the manuscript should be on the editor's desk. Emergencies happen. NEVER, NEVER miss a deadline or send it in late. One editor shared these words: "It's amazing that so many writers submit a query, which is accepted, but they never follow through with the manuscript. Plus, they never contact me about it being late—or that they can't take the assignment." By being a responsible writer, you can "always" find assignments. Never allow this to be a problem.
- If for some reason you have an emergency, offer a solution. Perhaps you could email the manuscript in one week. Or, perhaps the article could go in the next issue. Of course, this is the editor's decision.
- Avoid last minute changes. Everyone has a deadline—writers, editors, publishers, and printers. One person can hold up an entire production. If you're that person, do you think the editor will work with you again?

Tip # 5: When in Doubt...Ask

- Seek clarification about a part of the contract you don't understand. Do this weeks before the article is due—not the night before!

- Ask for editorial input. When discussing an idea or writing a query, I'll often ask the editor if there is information he would like included? Perhaps he has been thinking about this idea, but hasn't had time to write one. But here, you're a writer and have the assignment. Now is your time to be of service.

- Check for the current editor of the magazine. Some magazines have several department editors. Know the correct person. Check the *Writer's Market,* but realize this text may not be current information. Call the telephone number listed in the Writer's Market if unsure of the personnel.

Tip # 6. Don't Over-React to Edits

- What if changes were made to your article? Why? What can you learn from these changes?

- Realize the editor doesn't want to re-write. He has plenty to do without a full edit of your article.

- If an editor requests a re-write, follow up immediately.

- Respond by saying, "Of course, I'll rewrite. I want to be part of the team for your magazine. I want my article to be one that makes a difference in the lives of your readers—whether it's to inspire, educate, inform or entertain."

Tip # 7.: Tips for Removing Barriers

- Attend writing workshops.

- Learn from others.

- Pick up on current trends or themes.

- See the editor as a friend.

Networking Can Pay Off

Respond to the following statements or questions:

1. Why is networking important?

   _____

   _____

   _____

2. Contacts make a difference. List 3 ways. _____

   _____

   _____

3. How can you apply the Boy Scout motto: "Be Prepared" to writing?

   _____

   _____

   _____

4. Respond: Networking is a two-way street.._____

   _____

   _____

What Works for Me

- Always use the proper title (Mr. Ms. Mrs. or other titles)

- Avoid using the first name, such as "Dear Jane," until you know the person and the editor has used your first name in correspondence.

- Always document the sources and research you have used. This saves the copy-editor time. Plus, it's required of you, the writer.

- Send Christmas cards and other greetings when appropriate.

- Ask for prayer concerns that affect an editor's family. Share prayer needs for yourself. Treat an editor like you would want to be treated.

- Editors want to help you. They make our work, as writers, look good!

Do You See Networking as a Struggle or an Uphill Battle?

- It depends on "If you see your cup half-full or half-empty." When I taught at Union University, I often told my students: "Choose a career that you would love to get up and go to work on Monday morning!" I knew that if they were happy with their jobs, they would never work another day in their lives!

- Realize that writing is a competitive business. Other people are standing in line for writing contracts. How do your talents and skills stand out from others? Name three.

  1._____

  2._____

  3._____

Networking Can Help Promote Your Book

Most magazine editors are eager to help promote your book. However, the book must be a topic related to the publication and will relate to the reader. If your book meets these requirements, give the editor a copy, and ask her to write a review. Prepare a Writer's Bio, and other information that will enable the editor to complete this article without a lot of additional research.

Another way networking can help promote your book is through contacts. Do you have acquaintances in a civil club? A library? School or university? Your church? Offer to present a PowerPoint program that reviews your book. Most organizations offer an honorarium. If not, offer to present a free program. Ask them if you can sell your books there.

Distribute advertisements and handouts on your book to people you know. Use social media to network with friends and colleagues. Additional information on social networking will be available in another Boot Camp for Christian Writers Book.

The Secret Holocaust Diaries: The Untold Story of Nonna Bannister is in its 11th printing (as of Dec. 2012). Published in 2009, the book has won major awards, and has been translated in several languages. Part of the success comes from networking with friends, acquaintances, and even strangers. Personally, I've spoken to more than 150 different groups and organizations on this book.

Networking pays off. The cost is your time and efforts. These contacts make a difference in the success of your book or your writing.

What Does The Bible Say?

How can the Bible help us become better writers? Look at the following Scriptures.

About Faith

Now faith is being sure of what we hope for and certain of what we do not see.

~Hebrews 11:1

About Prayer

Be still before the Lord and wait patiently for him. ~Psalm 37:7

About Anxiety

Do not be anxious about anything, but in everything, by prayer and petition, with thanksgiving, present your requests to God. ~Philippians 4:6

About Guidance

Teach me to do your will, for you are my God. ~Psalm 143:10

*   *   *   *   *

Our Boot Camp for Christian Writers is made up of people who love to write—and people who love the Lord. We are a family. And families rejoice when there is a need for celebration. Families help each other in times of trouble. And families pray in times of sorrow. We welcome you to our unique family of writers!

Notes from Section III:

Appendices

Developing a Writing Career –The Seasons of Life

For years I searched for something to fulfill this creative energy that was part of my life. During childhood my artistic side flowed by designing clothes for paper dolls, and then moved into making doll clothes. Soon, I was making all my clothes and even sewed for others. Like a woven tapestry, this thread of creativity was part of who I was--part of my every thought, part of my being.

As a child, books intrigued me. So did a new tablet. I recall the excitement when I sharpen a new pencil for the first time. Or, open the first page of a new spiral-back writing tablet. It was something about that fresh, clean page that needed words to fill up the lines. Even the smell of a new tablet was exciting!

As I moved into the teen years, I entered the state fair where I won blue ribbons in sewing, flower arrangement, and embroidery. By this time, I was making almost all of my clothes. In fact, my homemade dresses measured up to those sold in any store. Perhaps that's because my mother insisted that the sewing be perfect. There was no room for "half-doing" anything. Mother often said, "If it's worth doing, it's worth doing right!"

Into my life comes Matt Tomlin, a young, handsome ministerial student. Marrying at age 18, I made not only my wedding dress—a beautiful long-white satin gown with a long veil, but all my trousseau—known as "going-away" clothes. I never understood why the term was used for leaving on a 3-day honeymoon. Especially, when we returned, we rented a small apartment only five miles from my parents' home.

Marrying young has advantages – and sometimes disadvantages. But looking back, I wouldn't change a thing. As a student-wife, I attended Union University with my husband. Matt served as pastor of a small country church. Driving over 2-

hours each Sunday, taught us to trust in God in unseen ways. Somehow the tires on our old car usually got us there and back each week. Between the produce from my parents' garden, his parents pitching in and a church pounding each Christmas, we survived. You understand the word "pounding," don't you? That's where the congregation brings sacks or pounds of food. Once we received 15, five-pound bags of sugar –plus, jars of canned green beans, tomatoes, jellies and pickles. How excited I was to fill our empty cabinets with all that wonderful food! Once again, imagination helped out when a meal consisted of a quart of home-canned tomatoes and spaghetti. Meat was a rare item. God provided.

Throughout my young adult years I tried numerous hobbies, projects and activities. Looking back, everything revolved around innovative ideas. I searched for something new. How could I use my creative talent in a resourceful way? How could I be inspired by the natural world God created? Fascinated by designing clothes for myself and our daughter, I scanned Vogue Magazines and window-shopped at the best boutiques for women and children. Flower design, using something worthless to others and turning it into a treasure for our home became a creative endeavor. I enjoyed the challenge of using simple ingredients to make delicious meals. Creativity was at work—only taking different paths.

Finding Mentors

But with all these projects and activities, I was still searching. Then, one day I read that LifeWay offered a Summer Writing Conference where people could learn how to write and publish. My husband, Matt, and I attended. There we met Bob Hastings, one of the speakers who later became my mentor. Bob was the editor of the Illinois Baptist Paper and was the author of many magazines articles and books. Readers will remember his *Tinyburg Tales*, a fictional place where all the women are strong, the men are good-looking and all the children are above average.

Bob introduced me to editors and wrote letters recommending me for writing and speaking assignments. One editor was Charlie Warren, editor of Home Life Magazine. After submitting my first article to Charlie, he said, "If you will let me help you, I believe you will be one of the writers we call on regularly." Do you recall having an elementary teacher take a red pencil and make numerous corrections on your paper? Well, that's exactly what Charlie did. He cut it to pieces! It dripped red ink! I'm sure he spent several hours making changes and showing me how I could rewrite and edit. I'll never forget his kindness to help a new writer.

And yes, I did return home from the writing conference with two assignments. But I was the only one—I think. That's because during the course of the workshop, we were told not to bother editors and never to go directly to their second floor office. Well, as soon as the speaker spoke these words, I headed upstairs. There are times when rules are meant to be broken. This was the time!

Teaching as a Way of Helping Others

I often recall those dedicated teachers who patiently taught me the mechanics of writing. Spanning from first-grade all the way through graduate school, these professionals have made a difference in my life and the lives of others. Teaching is like a circle with no end. What we give to others—they pass it along. I owe them a debt of gratitude.

Coming from a family of teachers, my mother, aunt, female cousins and friends, I, too, chose a career in education. After teaching kindergarten students in public school to being Assistant Professor of Education at Union University, in Jackson, Tennessee, I completed thirty-three years of professional work as grant writer for the Jackson-Madison County School in Jackson, TN. Although I was teaching others to write, I still searched for that special spark that wasn't part of my life. That is until I wrote and sold my first article in *Living with Teenagers*, a Christian magazine published by LifeWay. "How to Communicate with Your Teen" was accepted and published in 1989. Now at last, I was a published author and life has never been the same.

Creativity takes numerous forms. Like the seasons, we, too, change. Perhaps I wasn't ready to write-to-publish until I was 48-years-old. But I can't imagine my life without putting words on paper—now a computer—and using my original ideas to communicate with readers.

Recently a woman asked me how I wrote so many articles. My reply, "You only have to know the 26 letters of the alphabet and numbers 1 – 10 and you can write anything." Well, maybe there's a little more to writing than that, but you understand the idea.

About this time, I met Denise George at a writer's conference. Isn't it strange how God gives us opportunities and it's up us to take advantage of these events? Already seasoned writers, Denise and I took a break from the session and ended up on an outside porch. An editor had suggested I might like to meet this woman—whose name was Denise George from Birmingham. I looked at her—she looked at me—and we introduced ourselves. And from that time on, we've been best friends. God is good! He had a plan that would take us on a journey that neither of us could imagine!

Boot Camp for Christian Writers

Denise and I continued our writing ministry. Mine, mostly magazine articles, and Denise, books. People we met asked us questions, such as: How did you start writing? What makes a difference in receiving a contract instead of a rejection letter? How can I network with other writers and editors? How can I write to inspire, educate, inform and entertain others? How can I write to glorify God? Endless questions. Unknown answers that needed a response.

After asking God how we could help others know this passion that we possess, we decided to start a writing ministry for women, called "For Women Who Love to Write." After several weekend retreats, men starting requesting that they attend, also. To accommodate them, we started our Boot Camp for Christian Writers, an all-day event where we teach writing-to-publish.

By the year 2012, we've taught over 1,500 people to write-to-publish. Beeson Divinity School on the campus of Samford University in Birmingham, AL has generously provided support and space for our workshops. We are under the umbrella of the Lay Academy of Theology and promoted in Beeson mail-outs. In west Tennessee, Union University in Jackson, TN is working with us to offer Boot Camps for people in this area. Through various media, such as newspapers, radio and television interviews, we are contacting people. Churches sponsor those unable to attend. People telephone about future seminars. Interest runs high.

Each year, several Boot Camps are offered at Beeson. As the need for learning-to-write grows, other locations are being considered.

As we reach more people who have a dream of writing-to-publish, we pray that we can be an instrument in the hands of God. That we will give godly advice, encourage our Boot Campers and be supportive as they network with others.

Example of a Writer's Bio

Writer's Bio

Carolyn R. Tomlin

5 Greenway Drive

Jackson, TN 38305

Email: carolyn.tomlin@yahoo.com

Web page: www.carolyntomlin.com

Web page: www.BootCampforChristianWriters.com

Carolyn R.Tomlin has been in the field of education for over 33 years. During this time she was the director of a preschool program, a kindergarten and elementary teacher, Assistant Professor of Education at Union University, and retired in 2001 as the grant writer for the Jackson-Madison County School System. In four years she raised over $5.5 million dollars.

Mrs. Tomlin has combined her educational career with that of writing and photography. Since 1988 she has published 8 books and over 3,600 articles in the secular and Christian magazines, including: Journal Communications, Inc. (Bowling Green, KY; Jackson, TN Magazine, Images of Bartlett, TN, Asheville, NC, Dickson, TN), *American Profile, Entrepreneur, PTO Today, Today's School, Growing Edge, Tennessee Magazine, GRIT, Early Childhood News, The Kansas City Star* Newspaper, *Woodall Travel Magazines, Bus Tour Magazine, HomeLife, ParentLife, Mature Living* and others. *The Secret Holocaust Diaries: The Untold Story of Nonna Bannister,* published by Tyndale Publishers was published in April 2009 with co-author, Denise George. Recent books include: *What I Wish I'd Known Sooner: Parents* and *Teachers*, available as an e-book and printed edition with Amazon.com. and Barnes & Noble.

As a regular monthly columnist, she writes the "Parent Section" for *The City News* (Jackson, TN); Senior column for *Living Light News* (Canada)*;* "A Parent Speaks" for *The Baptist & Reflector,* "The Best of the Rest" for *Mature Living* and the "Home & School Connection" a newspaper columns for several area newspapers.

Tomlin is a frequent speaker for teacher/parent workshops and teaches writing conferences. During the 1990s she was an annual speaker or workshop leader for LifeWay Writers Workshop in Nashville in which she encouraged others to become published authors. As the co-owner of "Boot Camp for

Christian Writers," she teaches seminars with Denise George on writing-to-publish at Beeson Divinity School at Samford University in Birmingham. A frequent speaker at universities, civic clubs, women's Christian groups and libraries, Tomlin combines travel writing while teaching workshops in China, Russia, and the Caribbean,

Tomlin received a B.A. in Elementary Education from Union University, Jackson, TN; a M.Ed. in Elementary Education with a concentration in Early Childhood Ed, a certification in Supervision and Administration from the University of Memphis and has completed all course work for the Doctor of Education Degree.

She is a native of Jackson, Tennessee where she lives with her husband, Dr. Matt Tomlin, a Baptist minister. They are members of First Baptist Church, Jackson. The Tomlins have two children and six grandchildren. A red Pomeranian puppy chooses to share his life with the family.

Appendix 4

Activity Pages

Networking Suggestions for Writers

Personal contacts "do" make a difference. Put yourself in an editor's shoes. Brainstorm characteristics that would be a factor in giving a writer an assignment or a regular column.

1._____

2._____

3._____

4._____

5._____

Which characteristics could have a negative effect?

1._____

2._____

3._____

4._____

5._____

How should a writer respond to a letter of rejection?

1._____

2._____

3._____

Also by Carolyn Tomlin

The following books, in hardcopy, paperback, and as ebooks, can be ordered and/or downloaded through amazon.com as well as other outlets.

Boot Camp for Christian Writers Carolyn Tomlin Writing-To-Publish: The Basic Foundations 2

The Publishing Opportunities That Await You! Section I: In the first part of this book, I'll explain the type of articles in both the Christian and secular market that need your manuscript, work that will educate, encourage, entertain and inspire others through the written word! Learn editorial techniques for publishing, how to break into those markets, get your message across, and earn extra $$$.

The Basics of Article Publishing for Print Magazines & Online Magazines: Boot Camp for Christian Writers (Volume 4)

Use these as guidelines to write your own article. As an added bonus, I have included enrichment activities you can do at home or with a writing friend. Practice these activities and develop your skills as a writer. The book also has pages to write down your thoughts and ideas. I believe that writing is a gift given by God. He gives us this talent and it's up to us to learn the mechanics of putting words on paper. A Bible verse that has given me hope is Isaiah 40:31: "But those who hope in the Lord will renew their strength. They will soar on wings like eagles; they will run and not grow weary, they will walk and not be faint."

Four More Articles Editors Love and How to Write Them: Boot Camp for Christian Writers (Volume 6)

Includes: "Writing and Selling the How-to Article"
"Finding Markets for Newspaper and Mini-Columns"
"Breaking into Magazine Markets with Fillers"
"Seeing the World—Writing the Travel Article"

What I Wish I'd Known Sooner: Parents

Do you ever wish the things about being a parent hadn't taken you so long to learn? This book is part of a series and focuses on the joys of being a parent. Bits of wisdom the author learned from raising two children are interwoven with prayers. You'll laugh, and rejoice in this role of "Parenthood." Section two, The Home and School Connection, offers guidance and self-help for parents as they deal with school-related issues. You'll find answers to Bus Safety, Making Friends, Peer Pressure, How to Talk with the Teacher, and other topics.

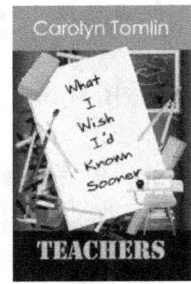

What I Wish I'd Known Sooner: Teachers

Part of a series, this book is written for educators. Included are bits of wisdom, prayers for teachers and students. Chapters are divided into areas affecting teachers, such as First Day of School, Open House, Bus Duty, and others. This series has been used in speaking to teacher groups, given as a gift and as a quick read for those who are able to laugh instead of cry when facing situations that arise in everyday life. Prayers give the reader strength and courage.

More Alike than Different
(story and coloring book)

By Carolyn Tomlin, illustrated by Ellen C. Maze

This is a story of Matthew, a young boy, who makes friends with children in his community from different cultures and ethnic groups. He soon learns that God made and loves all children and that we are all "more alike than different." Black and white line drawings provide a kinesthetic form of learning as children color the simple pictures.

The Secret Holocaust Diaries: The Untold Story of Nonna Bannister

by Nonna Bannister, Carolyn Tomlin and Denise George

Nonna Bannister almost carried a secret to her Tennessee grave. As the only known family survivor of the Holocaust, she came to America after the World War II, married Henry Bannister and did not tell him about being a Holocaust survivor for over forty years. Hidden under her dress, her grandmother tied a little ticking pillow filled with family photos. In this pillow, Nonna kept her secret. It's a true story of a little Russian girl who survived because of faith in God, love of family and the ability to forgive her enemies. This award-winning book was Published by *Tyndale House Publishers.*

The following books are out-of-print but may be available on www.half.com, www.amazon.com **or other outlets.**

Teachers as Published Writers

A practical guide to writing and publishing for teachers. Readers will learn how to know the magazine market, understand the reader's needs and sell ideas developed in the classroom. Other teachers will benefit from your ideas across the curriculum. Published by *Judy Wood Publishing Company.*

From the Cat's Point of View

Written for cat lovers, this book gives a glimpse inside the mind of our furry friends. Can cats read your mind? Do they relate to your emotions? Read looking at life through the eyes of a cat to discover more about yourself—as well as that of your feline. Published by *Judy Wood Publishing Company.*

More Alike than Different, (A children's story book)

Focusing on accepting multicultural differences, Matthew, a young boy meets the people in his neighborhood. Written as an easy-reader and as a listen-to-me book, children will soon be repeating the phrases uses over and over again. Published by *WMU Publishers.*

Mental Pause

Taking a humorous approach at menopause, the author describes emotions and behaviors related to this time in a woman's life. Published by *Judy Wood Publishing Company.*

True Tales or Tall Tales: You Decide with Denise George and Carolyn Tomlin

Some stories are just too strange to be true—or are they? Based on stories from the news and the writer's creativity, you will not know if this is a true story or a tall tale. Turn to the back of the book to find the answer. Written for upper elementary and middle school students. Published by *Judy Wood Publishing Company.*

105 Ways to Use Index Cards and Sticky Notes in the Classroom,
Judy Wood and Carolyn Tomlin

This book offers suggestions for using index cards and sticky notes in all areas of the curriculum—from reading, math, science, social studies and others. Published by *Judy Wood Publishing Company*.

A Parent's Guide to Summer Survival

School's out! The long-awaited summer vacation has finally arrived. For most kids, it's approximately 10 weeks (or 70 days, or 1,680 hours) each summer. For students, nothing could be better. For parents, what will you do with the kids all day? Instead of fussing, being bored, or having a "panic attack" try some of the great ideas in this book. Published by *Judy Wood Publishing Company*.

365 Email Messages for Students and Teachers (with Veronica Coulston)

Make using the Internet and Email fun for students! Teachers find questions from the curriculum based on history, fine arts, sports, literature, social studies, science and other topics. Each day they email their class a question. The student must find the answer by using the Internet. Or, students can post the question for their peers. This is a fun way to learn, as well as master using the Internet and email. Published by *Judy Wood Publishing Company*.

The Tutor's Handbook: Math (Grade 2)

This helpful guide offers enrichment for students and includes: a sample tutoring session, creative tutoring strategies, reproducible work sheets and real-life math connections. Published by *Frank Schaffer Publications*.

First Steps in Missions, Vol. 6 with Tammie Worsham

Activities and ideas for Mission Friends and Teachers. This book offers fun and learning-based activities for home-schoolers, Vacation Bible Clubs, Christian schools and others.
Published by Woman's Missionary Union

About the Author

Carolyn Tomlin has been writing and published since 1988. She has authored 18 books and over 4,000 magazine articles in magazines such as *Entrepreneur, Kansas City News, American Profile, Home Life, Mature Living, ParentLife*, and many others. She and Denise George are writing 14 books for the popular seminar, Boot Camp for Christian Writers. Her latest books are *What I Wish I'd Known Sooner: Parents, What I Wish I'd Known Sooner: Teachers* and *More Alike Than Different* (a story and coloring book for children.). Carolyn is married to Dr. Matt Tomlin, a Southern Baptist pastor. They have two adult children, Cindy Tomlin Coulston and Kevin Tomlin and six grandchildren.

You may contact Carolyn Tomlin at:
Carolyn's email address: Carolyn.tomlin@yahoo.com
Web Page: www.carolyntomlin.com
For writers: http://christianwritersbootcamp.blogspot.com
Beeson's website:
http://www.beesondivinity.com/bootcampforchristianwriters
Connect with Carolyn Tomlin on Facebook.

Boot Camp for Christian Writers®

Boot Camp for Christian Writers® is a no-nonsense, basic, information-packed, series of all-day, one-day seminars that educate and equip Christian writers to write clearly, communicate effectively to a chosen audience, professionally approach magazine editors and book publishers with good ideas, and get articles and books published!

Founded in February, 2009, by Denise George and Carolyn Tomlin, Boot Camp for Christian Writers® is based on Colossians 3:12-17 and (Col. 3:23-24): "Whatever you do, work at it with all your heart, as working for the Lord, not for men... It is the Lord Christ you are serving."

George and Tomlin keep in close touch with their Boot Campers through email, and are available to answer questions, give advice, etc. Boot Campers can communicate with each other through the Boot Camp FaceBook Page. The Boot Camper Blogspot provides regular information on writing, tips, publishing trends, current writing news, photos, etc.

George and Tomlin teach using three modes of learning:

1. Visual: They offer the latest in technology with creative PowerPoint and KeyNote presentations;
2. Auditory: They present information in a comfortable classroom-style setting, and give question & answer opportunities after each seminar;
3. Kinesthetic: They provide printed handout materials to go along with their presentations, as well as personally-written books (like this one) that participants can purchase to gain deeper understanding, further information, and self-learning exercises to use at home.

Hundreds of people have already participated in these information-packed seminars! The seminars are exciting and fun, and writers enjoy meeting each other and comparing ideas! Our Boot Campers are writing confidently, contacting editors with magazine and book ideas, selling articles to magazines, and receiving book contracts from major publishers! They are also learning how to self-publish and promote their books to the world! Attend one of the Boot Camp for Christian Writers® seminars and become a lifetime member of the "Family of Christian Writers."

Happy writing and may God bless you!

~ Carolyn Tomlin

Your Seminar Notes:

www.ingramcontent.com/pod-product-compliance
Lightning Source LLC
Chambersburg PA
CBHW080304290526
45790CB00005B/1929